BIOGRAPHY

BILL BAILEY

The Inspiring Story of His Remarkable Journey Through Comedy, Music, And Beyond

Kristin J. James

COPYRIGHT © 2024 KRISTIN J. JAMES

All rights reserved. Without the publisher's prior written consent, no portion of this publication may be copied, distributed, or transmitted in any way, including by photocopying, recording, or other mechanical or electronic means, with the exception of brief quotations used in critical reviews and other noncommercial uses allowed by copyright law.

TABLE OF CONTENTS

INTRODUCTION 5

CHAPTER ONE 10

    THE EARLY YEARS OF BILL BAILEY 10

    Education and Early Interests 11

    The Birth of "Bill" 13

    Early Career Beginnings 15

    The Rubber Bishops and a Budding Style: 16

    Solo Endeavors and Early Challenges 17

    Breakthrough and Recognition 18

CHAPTER TWO 21

    BILL BAILEY'S MUSICAL JOURNEY 21

    Musical Influences and Genres 23

    Band and Collaborative Projects 26

    Notable Performances and Contributions 27

    Favorite Stand-Up Moments 29

CHAPTER THREE 37

TELEVISION AND FILM APPEARANCES 37

CHAPTER FOUR **57**

LIVE PERFORMANCES AND TOURS 57

Bill Bailey's Tours: A Global Journey of Comedy and Music 61

Unique Aspects of Bill Bailey's Tours 70

CHAPTER FIVE **72**

PERSONAL LIFE 72

Hobbies and Interests 73

Bill Bailey's Political Views 78

Philanthropy and Activism 79

CHAPTER SIX **87**

A CAREER CROWNED WITH RECOGNITION 87

Bill Bailey's Influence on British Comedy and Stand-Up Culture 91

CHAPTER SEVEN **97**

QUOTES AND CAPTIVATING FACTS 97

Captivating Facts About Bill Bailey 100

CONCLUSION 105

INTRODUCTION

When I first encountered Bill Bailey, it was during one of his performances at the Edinburgh Festival Fringe. I remember the room buzzing with anticipation, a mix of both seasoned fans and curious newcomers, all eager to see the man who had carved out a unique niche in the world of comedy. As he stepped onto the stage, his long hair and ever-present, mischievous grin immediately drew us in. Within moments, he had the entire audience captivated, effortlessly blending wit with an extraordinary musical talent, demonstrating why he is considered one of the most innovative and beloved comedians of our time.

Bill Bailey, born Mark Robert Bailey on January 13, 1965, in Bath, Somerset, England, is a multifaceted entertainer known for his trademark long hair, beard, and distinctive style, Bailey seamlessly merges stand-up comedy with musical virtuosity. From an early age, Bailey exhibited a prodigious talent for music, learning to play the piano and guitar with remarkable proficiency. His father was a medical practitioner, and his mother a hospital ward sister, a background that perhaps influenced his keen observational humor and sharp intellect.

Bailey's deep love for music at an early age would later become a cornerstone of his comedic identity. He attended King Edward's School in Bath, where he was a standout student, excelling in both academics and extracurricular activities. It was here that he was given the nickname **"Bill"** by his music teacher, in reference to the famous song "Won't You Come Home Bill Bailey." His talent in music was evident from a young age, leading him to study at the prestigious London College of Music. Despite his aptitude, Bailey's career path took a turn towards comedy, a field where he could merge his musical skills with his sharp sense of humor.

Bailey began his journey in comedy with the group **The Rubber Bishops**, where he developed his craft alongside fellow comedian **Martin Stubbs**. His unique approach quickly set him apart; he was not just a comedian who could play an instrument, but a musician who could weave humor through melodies and lyrics, often using music to accentuate his comedic punchlines. His breakthrough came with the one-man show **"Bill Bailey's Cosmic Jam,"** which showcased his eclectic mix of musical parodies, surreal humor, and intelligent observations.

Over the years, Bailey's career has spanned various mediums, from stand-up and television to film and theatre. He gained widespread acclaim for his role as Manny in the British sitcom "Black Books," where his comedic chemistry with co-stars Dylan Moran and Tamsin Greig won him a new legion of fans. His television work also includes notable appearances on panel shows such **as "Never Mind the Buzzcocks"** and **"QI,"** where his quick wit and encyclopedic knowledge of music and obscure facts made him a favorite among audiences.

Bailey's stage performances are legendary, often described as a blend of stand-up, concert, and philosophical discourse. His shows like "Part Troll," "Tinselworm," and "Dandelion Mind" are celebrated for their intricate musical compositions, which range from classical parodies to heavy metal riffs, interspersed with his characteristic surreal humor and astute social commentary. He has the rare ability to make audiences laugh while simultaneously challenging them to think critically about the world around them.

In addition to his comedy and music, Bailey is an avid naturalist and passionate advocate for wildlife conservation. This interest has led him to participate in various television documentaries and campaigns aimed at raising awareness about environmental issues. His love for nature is often reflected in his work, where he seamlessly integrates themes of ecology and biodiversity, further enriching his performances with a depth of knowledge and genuine concern for the planet.

Let's unlock the world of Bill Bailey, the remarkable entertainer. We will journey through his rise to comedic fame, dissect his one-of-a-kind blend of stand-up and music, and dive into his relentless dedication to protecting our planet. ***Fasten your seatbelts, because with Bill Bailey, the journey is always surprising!***

CHAPTER ONE

THE EARLY YEARS OF BILL BAILEY

Mark Robert Bailey, widely known as Bill Bailey, was born on January 13, 1965, in Bath, Somerset. His upbringing in a modest yet intellectually stimulating environment significantly shaped his eclectic personality and multifaceted talents. Raised in Keynsham, a town nestled between Bath and Bristol, Bailey's early years were marked by a blend of medical professionalism, artistic exposure, and a supportive family environment.

Bill Bailey was the son of Christopher and Madryn Bailey. His father, Christopher Bailey, was an NHS general practitioner who ran a small surgery from the front of their home, providing healthcare to the local community. This setup not only demonstrated a dedication to service but also introduced young Bill to the concept of helping others. His mother, Madryn Bailey, worked as a hospital ward nurse, embodying compassion and dedication in her professional life. This combination of medical and caregiving professions in his household likely instilled in Bill a sense of responsibility and empathy, traits that would influence his comedic style and public persona.

Living next door to his maternal grandparents, Bill developed a close bond with his stonemason grandfather. This influence might explain his later appreciation for detail and craftsmanship, evident in his meticulously crafted stand-up routines. His mother's career in nursing could have also instilled in him a strong sense of empathy and observation, essential tools for any comedian.

Education and Early Interests

Bailey attended King Edward's School, an independent school in Bath, where he initially excelled academically. His early academic prowess suggested a promising future in traditional fields, but his interests soon began to diverge. Around the age of 15, Bailey discovered the thrill of performance, which marked a turning point in his life. He joined a school band called Behind Closed Doors, where he played original compositions, highlighting his early inclination towards creativity and originality.

His passion for music was further evidenced by his dedication to his studies in this field. He was the only student at his school to pursue A-level music, which he completed with an A grade. This achievement underscored his exceptional talent and commitment to music. His classical training laid a solid foundation for his future work, allowing him to incorporate a wide range of musical styles into his comedy.

Bailey's versatility extended beyond academics and music. He was also a talented sportsman, captaining the KES 2nd XI cricket team in 1982. His ability to balance sports and music often surprised his teachers, illustrating his multifaceted interests and talents. He was known for leading the singing on long coach trips back from away rugby fixtures, blending his love for music and camaraderie.

The Birth of "Bill"

It was during his school years that Bailey acquired the nickname "Bill." This moniker was given to him by his music teacher, who was impressed by Bailey's rendition of the song "Won't You Come Home Bill Bailey" on the guitar. The name stuck and would eventually become the moniker under which he would achieve fame.

After completing his schooling, Bailey embarked on higher education with a focus on English at Westfield College, part of the University of London. However, he left after a year, indicating an early realization that his true passions lay elsewhere. Despite this, his time at university was not wasted. He continued to cultivate his musical skills and obtained an Associate Diploma from the London College of Music, further solidifying his musical credentials.

Bailey's early performance career was marked by a variety of roles and experiences. He performed with a boy band called **The Famous Five**, an endeavor that allowed him to develop his stage presence and performance skills. His acting talents were also showcased in a stage production by the **Workers' Revolutionary Party**, titled **The Printers**, where he acted alongside renowned performers Vanessa Redgrave and Frances de la Tour. These early experiences in both music and acting were crucial in shaping his unique comedic style, which seamlessly blended musical virtuosity with sharp, observational humor.

Bill Bailey's upbringing and early years were marked by a blend of intellectual rigor, artistic exploration, and supportive family dynamics. Growing up in Keynsham, with the dual influences of his parents' medical professions and his grandparents' craftsmanship, Bailey developed a unique perspective on life. His education at King Edward's School, coupled with his early forays into music and performance, laid the groundwork for his future career. The nickname "Bill," given during his school years, became synonymous with his identity as a performer, encapsulating the blend of humor, music, and intellectual curiosity that defines his work. As Bailey transitioned into adulthood, his diverse experiences and talents converged, setting the stage for a career that would captivate audiences around the world.

Early Career Beginnings

Bill Bailey's journey to becoming a household name in the world of comedy began with a series of collaborations, solo performances, and the gradual development of his unique comedic style. His early career was characterized by perseverance, creative experimentation, and a relentless pursuit of his passion despite numerous challenges. Fresh out of university, Bill hit the road, touring the country alongside established comedians like **Mark Lamarr.** This early exposure to the live comedy circuit undoubtedly refined his performance skills and provided valuable insights into the world he was about to enter.

The Rubber Bishops and a Budding Style:

In 1984, Bailey formed a double act known as the **Rubber Bishops** with **Toby Longworth**, a fellow former pupil from King Edward's School in Bath. This partnership was a significant milestone in Bailey's early career. The Rubber Bishops allowed Bailey to experiment with integrating music into his comedy routines, a signature element that would define his later work. One of their memorable bits involved a joke about amoebas changing a lightbulb, showcasing Bailey's penchant for combining scientific humor with absurdity.

However, the Rubber Bishops faced a setback when Toby Longworth left the act in 1989 to join the Royal Shakespeare Company (RSC). This departure could have stalled Bailey's career, but he found a new partner in **Martin Stubbs.** The duo continued to perform together until Stubbs decided to pursue a more serious career, leaving Bailey at another crossroads.

Solo Endeavors and Early Challenges

The early 1990s were a period of both struggle and creative growth for Bailey. In 1994, he teamed up with **Sean Lock** to perform "Rock" at the Edinburgh Festival Fringe. This show, about an aging rockstar and his roadie, was script-edited by comedy writer Jim Miller and later serialized for the Mark Radcliffe show on BBC Radio 1. Despite the creative efforts, the show struggled with low attendance, with one notable performance attended solely by comedian Dominic Holland. This challenging period almost led Bailey to abandon his comedy career in favor of a **telesales job.**

Undeterred, Bailey decided to strike out on his own. In 1995, he launched his solo show, **Bill Bailey's Cosmic Jam**. This one-man show marked a significant turning point in his career. It allowed Bailey to fully express his unique comedic vision, seamlessly blending his musical talent with his whimsical and often surreal humor. The show was recorded at the Bloomsbury Theatre in London and broadcast in 1997 on Channel 4 as a one-hour special titled Bill Bailey Live. Though the special initially aired in an edited form, it was later released uncut on DVD in 2005 under its original title, Bill Bailey's Cosmic Jam.

Breakthrough and Recognition

Bailey's perseverance began to pay off. In 1995, he supported comedian Donna McPhail and subsequently won a Time Out award, recognizing his growing prominence in the comedy circuit. This award was a significant boost to his confidence and visibility.

Bailey returned to the **Edinburgh Festival Fringe** in 1996 with a new show that garnered critical acclaim and a nomination for the prestigious **Perrier Comedy Award**. This nomination placed him in the company of other rising stars, including **Dylan Moran**, who narrowly edged him out in one of the closest votes in the award's history. The nomination was a result of Bailey's evolving comedic prowess and his ability to captivate audiences with his innovative style.

The late 1990s saw Bailey solidifying his place in the comedy world. In 1999, he won the **Best Live Stand-Up award** at the **British Comedy Awards**. This accolade was a recognition of his unique ability to entertain and engage audiences with his eclectic mix of music, satire, and observational humor.

Bailey's success was not just limited to the stage. His performances and innovative approach to comedy caught the attention of television producers, leading to more opportunities in TV and radio. His ability to tie together music and postmodern gags with his whimsical, rambling style became his trademark, endearing him to a broad audience and setting the stage for future successes in his career.

Bill Bailey's early career was marked by a series of collaborations, solo performances, and a relentless drive to establish himself in the competitive world of comedy. From his touring days with Mark Lamarr to the formation of the Rubber Bishops, and from the challenges faced during the Edinburgh Festival Fringe to the success of Bill Bailey's Cosmic Jam, Bailey's journey was characterized by perseverance, creativity, and a unique comedic vision. His ability to blend music with humor, coupled with his intellectual and whimsical style, eventually earned him critical acclaim and a dedicated following, paving the way for his continued success in comedy and beyond.

CHAPTER TWO

BILL BAILEY'S MUSICAL JOURNEY

Bill Bailey's career as a musician is as multifaceted and dynamic as his comedic pursuits. His ability to blend humor with music has set him apart in the entertainment world, making him a unique and innovative performer. With a wide array of musical skills, perfect pitch, and an eclectic range of influences, Bailey has built a distinctive style that appeals to a broad audience.

Bill boasts an impressive musical arsenal. Keyboards, guitars, and the theremin are just a few of the tools at his disposal. But his musical curiosity extends beyond the conventional. He breathes life into instruments like the kazoo and bongo drums, injecting unexpected sounds and rhythms into his comedic narratives. His ability to play the clarinet to Grade 6 standard shows a commitment to musical discipline, even as he pushes boundaries in his comedic performances.

He incorporates these skills seamlessly into his stand-up routines, enhancing his comedy with musical interludes that range from the absurd to the profoundly musical.

Keyboard: Bailey's ability with the keyboard is exceptional, allowing him to traverse genres from classical to jazz and rock. His performances often include intricate keyboard pieces that showcase his technical skill and musicality.

Guitar: The guitar is central to Bailey's musical identity. He skillfully uses it for various comedic effects, from rock parodies to classical adaptations. His guitar work is not just limited to background music; it often takes center stage in his routines.

Theremin: An unusual choice, the theremin adds a layer of eccentricity to Bailey's performances. His use of this instrument, which is played without physical contact, underscores his inventive approach to music and comedy.

Kazoo and Bongos: These instruments provide comic relief and are used to punctuate jokes or enhance musical sketches. Bailey's ability to integrate them into his acts demonstrates his versatility and creativity.

Clarinet: Bailey has achieved Grade 6 on the clarinet, indicating a high level of proficiency. Although not as frequently showcased as other instruments, his clarinet skills add to his diverse musical repertoire.

Musical Influences and Genres

Blessed with perfect pitch, Bill possesses a natural ear for music. This allows him to flawlessly execute complex melodies while simultaneously deconstructing them for comedic effect. His musical influences are as diverse as his instrument collection. Jazz, rock (particularly the progressive rock of the 70s), and even drum and bass find their way into his stand-up routines. He is not afraid to experiment with classical music either, reimagining familiar pieces with a comedic twist.

Bailey's musical influences are broad, encompassing a variety of genres that he incorporates into his comedy:

Jazz: Bailey's jazz influences are evident in his improvisational skills and his ability to navigate complex musical structures. He often uses jazz to create humorous and sophisticated musical interludes.

Rock and Prog Rock: Particularly drawn to progressive rock from the early seventies, Bailey's rock influences are a staple of his performances. His parodies and covers of rock classics are both nostalgic and humorous.

Drum'n'Bass: This genre's rhythmic complexity and energetic beats provide a dynamic backdrop for Bailey's comedy. His use of drum'n'bass highlights his ability to adapt contemporary music styles into his acts.

Classical Music: Bailey's classical training is evident in his performances, where he often includes classical pieces with a comedic twist. His perfect pitch allows him to perform these pieces with precision and humor.

Theme Songs and Parodies: Bailey's talent for creating musical parodies of popular theme songs is a hallmark of his act. Whether it is performing "The Star-Spangled Banner" in a minor key or reinterpreting the Hokey Cokey in the style of Kraftwerk, his ability to transform familiar tunes into comedic gold is unmatched.

Bill's true genius lies in using music to enhance his comedic message. Imagine a rendition of the Star-Spangled Banner played in a minor key or a hilarious reinterpretation of the Hokey Cokey in the style of electronic pioneer Kraftwerk. These musical parodies are more than just background entertainment – they become punchlines themselves, adding a new layer of humor to his observations.

Band and Collaborative Projects

Bailey's musical journey includes significant collaborative efforts, highlighting his ability to work with other musicians and comedians:

Beergut 100: Founded in 1995 with comedy writer Jim Miller, Beergut 100 was a punk band that also featured Martin Trenaman, Phil Whelans, and Kevin Eldon as the lead singer. The band performed at various venues, including the 2006 Edinburgh Festival Fringe, blending punk music with comedic performances.

Cosmic Shindig: In February 2007, Bailey performed with the BBC Concert Orchestra and Anne Dudley in a show titled Cosmic Shindig. The performance featured orchestrally accompanied versions of Bailey's songs, an exploration of orchestral instruments, and new musical pieces. This collaboration was broadcast on BBC Radio 3 as part of Comic Relief 2007.

Remarkable Guide to the Orchestra: In October 2008, Bailey performed "Bill Bailey's Remarkable Guide to the Orchestra" at the Royal Albert Hall with the BBC Concert Orchestra, conducted by Anne Dudley. This show was a significant milestone, blending educational elements with comedy and showcasing Bailey's deep understanding of orchestral music.

Notable Performances and Contributions

Bailey's musical journey is marked by several notable performances and contributions to the music and comedy scenes:

Private Passions: In November 2009, Bailey appeared as a guest on "Private Passions," a biographical music discussion program on BBC Radio 3. This appearance allowed him to discuss his musical influences and share his eclectic taste with a broader audience.

Sonisphere Festival: In July 2011, Bailey headlined the Saturn Stage at the Sonisphere Festival in Knebworth. This performance was notable for its heavy metal influences and showcased Bailey's ability to adapt his comedy to different musical genres. He later released an album, "In Metal," featuring songs from his Sonisphere performance.

Eurovision Ambition: Encouraged by fan petitions, Bailey considered putting himself forward as Britain's entry for the Eurovision Song Contest in 2008. Although this plan did not come to fruition, it highlighted his popularity and the public's appreciation for his musical talent.

Music House for Children: In June 2014, Bailey became a patron of The Music House for Children, alongside Sophie Ellis-Bextor, in celebration of the organization's 20th anniversary. This role reflects his commitment to supporting music education and nurturing young talent.

Bill's musical ambitions have reached orchestral heights. He collaborated with the BBC Concert Orchestra and composer Anne Dudley on a show titled "Cosmic Shindig." This project saw some of his most popular comedic songs reimagined with orchestral arrangements, showcasing the surprising depth and complexity of his musical compositions. It wasn't a one-time event; he went on to perform "Bill Bailey's Remarkable Guide to the Orchestra" at the Royal Albert Hall, further blurring the lines between comedy and classical music.

Favorite Stand-Up Moments

Bill Bailey's stand-up career is studded with unforgettable moments and legendary routines that have endeared him to audiences worldwide. His unique blend of musical talent, surreal humor, and intellectual humor makes his performances memorable and distinctive.

The Minor Key "Star-Spangled Banner"

One of Bailey's most famous routines involves performing the American national anthem, "The Star-Spangled Banner," in a minor key. This routine exemplifies his ability to take a familiar piece of music and transform it into something entirely new and humorous. By altering the anthem's key, Bailey creates a somber and haunting version that contrasts sharply with its usual patriotic fervor. This performance not only showcases Bailey's musical prowess but also his knack for finding humor in unexpected places.

The Hokey Cokey in the Style of Kraftwerk

Bailey's rendition of the Hokey Cokey in the style of the electronic band Kraftwerk is another legendary routine. By reimagining this simple children's song as an electronic, robotic performance, Bailey highlights his talent for musical parody. He dons a deadpan expression and adopts Kraftwerk's minimalist aesthetic, using synthesizers to create a humorous and surreal reinterpretation of the Hokey Cokey. This routine is a fan favorite, demonstrating Bailey's ability to blend music and comedy seamlessly.

Classical Music with a Twist

Bailey's classical music routines are a staple of his stand-up performances. One particularly memorable moment is his interpretation of Beethoven's "Für Elise," which he performs as a reggae tune. This unexpected twist on a classical piece not only showcases Bailey's versatility as a musician but also his inventive comedic mind. By juxtaposing the refined elegance of classical music with the laid-back rhythms of reggae, Bailey creates a delightful and humorous musical experience.

The Pub Pianist

In one of his stand-up specials, Bailey performs a routine about a pub pianist who is unable to stop playing once he starts. The pianist, played by Bailey, continuously transitions from one piece of music to another, incorporating various styles and genres. This routine highlights Bailey's improvisational skills and his ability to engage the audience through music. The relentless nature of the pub pianist's performance becomes increasingly absurd, culminating in a hilarious and musically rich spectacle.

Middle-Class Musical Gangster Rap

Bailey's parody of gangster rap from a middle-class perspective is a standout routine that pokes fun at the incongruity between the aggressive style of rap and the genteel nature of middle-class life. In this routine, Bailey raps about mundane middle-class concerns, such as gardening and shopping at Waitrose, using the hard-hitting beats and rhythms of traditional gangster rap. This juxtaposition creates a comedic tension that resonates with audiences, showcasing Bailey's sharp social satire and his ability to cross cultural boundaries with humor.

The Evolution of Dance Music

Bailey's exploration of the evolution of dance music is a routine that combines historical insight with musical parody. He takes the audience on a journey through different eras of dance music, from the 1970s disco era to contemporary electronic dance music (EDM). Bailey demonstrates the distinctive features of each genre, often exaggerating them for comedic effect. His ability to mimic various musical styles and his commentary on the changing nature of dance music make this routine both educational and entertaining.

The Insect Nation

In his "Insect Nation" routine, Bailey imagines a world where insects have formed their own society and culture. He creates an elaborate and humorous narrative, complete with insect leaders, cultural practices, and even insect pop music. This routine showcases Bailey's talent for storytelling and his ability to create vivid, imaginative worlds. The absurdity of an insect civilization, combined with Bailey's detailed descriptions and musical interludes, makes this routine a standout in his repertoire.

The One-Man Techno Band

Bailey's one-man techno band routine is a technical and comedic tour de force. Using a loop pedal and various electronic instruments, Bailey creates complex techno music live on stage. He builds layers of beats and melodies, demonstrating his skill as a musician and his understanding of electronic music production. The routine culminates in a high-energy techno track, with Bailey dancing and interacting with the audience. This performance is a testament to Bailey's innovative approach to comedy and music, blending the two seamlessly to create a unique live experience.

Part Troll

"Part Troll" is one of Bailey's most celebrated stand-up shows, featuring a variety of his legendary routines. The show includes musical parodies, surreal humor, and sharp social commentary. One of the highlights is Bailey's critique of modern technology and consumer culture, delivered through humorous anecdotes and musical interludes. "Part Troll" is a comprehensive showcase of Bailey's talents, capturing the essence of his comedic and musical style.

Bill Bailey's Remarkable Guide to the Orchestra

In "Bill Bailey's Remarkable Guide to the Orchestra," Bailey collaborates with the BBC Concert Orchestra to explore the world of orchestral music through a comedic lens. This performance combines educational elements with Bailey's trademark humor, making classical music accessible and entertaining. He introduces the audience to various instruments, often with humorous descriptions and demonstrations. This show highlights Bailey's deep appreciation for music and his ability to communicate complex ideas in a fun and engaging way.

En Route to Normal

"En Route to Normal" is another of Bailey's acclaimed stand-up shows, featuring a mix of new material and classic routines. In this show, Bailey reflects on the absurdities of modern life, from the impact of technology to the quirks of human behavior. His musical routines in this show are as inventive as ever, including a mash-up of popular songs and original compositions. "En Route to Normal" exemplifies Bailey's ability to stay relevant and continue evolving as a performer.

The Cosmic Shindig

In "The Cosmic Shindig," Bailey performs with the BBC Concert Orchestra, blending orchestral music with his unique brand of comedy. This show includes orchestrally accompanied versions of Bailey's songs, explorations of different musical instruments, and new musical pieces. The collaboration with Anne Dudley and the BBC Concert Orchestra adds a layer of sophistication to

Bailey's performance, making it a memorable and musically rich experience.

CHAPTER THREE

TELEVISION AND FILM APPEARANCES

Bill Bailey's career has spanned numerous television shows and films, establishing him as a versatile performer. His comedic talent, combined with his musical prowess, has made him a beloved figure in both mediums. From his early days in children's television to his iconic roles in sitcoms and appearances on panel shows, Bailey's body of work showcases his wide-ranging abilities and unique comedic style.

Bailey's first television appearance was on the children's show Motormouth in the late 1980s, where he played piano for a mind-reading dog. Although a humble beginning, this quirky role hinted at Bailey's future in combining music with comedy. He later reminisced about this experience on the BBC show Room 101 with Paul Merton in

2000, showcasing his ability to find humor in his early career moments.

Is It Bill Bailey?

In 1998, following his nomination for the Perrier Comedy Award in 1996, the BBC gave Bailey his own television show, Is It Bill Bailey?. This show marked a significant milestone as it was the first time Bailey wrote and presented his own material. Is It Bill Bailey? featured a mix of surreal sketches, musical parodies, and stand-up routines, encapsulating Bailey's eclectic comedic style. Although it ran for only one season, Is It Bill Bailey? solidified his reputation as a unique and innovative comedian.

The show's format allowed Bailey to explore his comedic range fully. He blended traditional stand-up with elaborate musical interludes and absurd sketches. One notable sketch involved a parody of a public service announcement, complete with a deadpan delivery and a twist of surreal humor, characteristic of Bailey's style. Despite its short run, the show was influential in establishing Bailey's career and showcasing his ability to blend music and comedy in innovative ways.

Guest Appearances and Spaced Out Adventures:

The late 1990s weren't solely about his own show. Bill cemented his status as a comedic talent in high demand with a string of memorable guest appearances. Audiences delighted in his quick wit and absurdist observations on shows like "Have I Got News for You," a satirical news quiz show, and "Room 101," a panel show where guests attempt to convince the host why certain pet hates should be consigned to the titular room. Bill's appearances were often characterized by his offbeat humor and ability to riff off the moment, leaving audiences in stitches.

Bill's comedic talents were not restricted to panel shows. He also dabbled in the world of sitcoms with a memorable three-episode stint on the cult classic "Spaced." This quirky sitcom, created by and starring Simon Pegg and Jessica Stevenson, explored the lives of a group of twenty-something flatmates. Bill's portrayal of Bilbo Bagshot, the eccentric comic-shop manager, was a hilarious addition to the show's ensemble cast. Bilbo's love of obscure comics, conspiracy theories, and his endearing awkwardness resonated with audiences and cemented Bill's reputation for playing endearingly oddball characters.

Black Books: A Match Made in Sitcom Heaven:

Fate intervened in 1998 when Dylan Moran, a rising star in the British comedy scene, approached Bill with the pilot script for "Black Books." The premise was simple: a grumpy bookstore owner named Bernard Black (played by Moran) with a penchant for wine and a disdain for most customers, his hapless assistant Manny Bianco (played by Bill), and their socially awkward friend Fran (played by Tamsin Greig) navigate the chaotic world of running a bookshop. What unfolded was a hilarious and surprisingly touching sitcom that garnered a devoted cult following.

Bill's portrayal of Manny Bianco was a revelation. Manny, with his childlike optimism, enthusiasm for terrible puns, and unwavering loyalty to Bernard, was the perfect foil to Bernard's cynicism. Their odd-couple dynamic was a cornerstone of the show's humor, and Bill and Dylan's comedic chemistry was undeniable. Black Books also provided a platform for Bill to showcase his musical talents. The show featured several memorable musical moments, including a fantasy sequence where Manny envisions himself as a rockstar and a recurring gag where Bernard attempts (and fails) to play the recorder.

"Black Books" ran for three successful seasons, from 2000 to 2004. Although a short-lived sitcom, it left a lasting impression on British comedy. It won numerous awards, including a BAFTA for Best Situation Comedy, and is still fondly remembered by fans worldwide. Bill's portrayal of Manny Bianco is considered one of his most iconic roles, and "Black Books" serves as a testament to his ability to thrive in a scripted format and shine alongside another comedic genius.

Never Mind the Buzzcocks: From Panelist to Team Captain

Bill's comedic talents continued to flourish on television beyond "Black Books." In 2002, he landed a coveted role as a team captain on the popular music quiz show "Never Mind the Buzzcocks," succeeding Sean Hughes. His dry wit and quirky observations were a perfect fit for the show's fast-paced and often nonsensical humor. He quickly established himself as a fan favorite, bringing a unique energy to the panel discussions.

Bill's team captaincy was not just about delivering witty remarks and scoring points. He possessed an uncanny ability to weave obscure trivia and historical anecdotes into the music quiz format, often leaving his teammates and opponents bewildered yet strangely entertained. This willingness to veer off on comedic tangents and explore unexpected byways of musical knowledge became a hallmark of his time on the show.

However, his tenure was not without its comedic barbs. Host Mark Lamarr playfully teased Bill about his unconventional appearance and his fascination with wildlife, particularly woodland animals. This playful rivalry became a running gag on the show, adding another layer of amusement for viewers. Bill would often counter with self-deprecating humor or witty rejoinders about Lamarr's own sartorial choices, keeping the banter lighthearted and humorous.

By 2008, Bill decided to step down from "Never Mind the Buzzcocks" after a six-year run. While his departure was met with disappointment by fans, Bill later jokingly attributed his decision to a growing frustration with the show's increasing focus on mainstream pop music. He playfully remarked that he was tired of humming Britney Spears' "Toxic" to obscure indie music figures who may not have even heard the song. This comment highlighted Bill's preference for alternative and unconventional music, a taste that often clashed with the show's pop-centric format. Bill also mentioned feeling a desire to take a break from the repetitive nature of panel shows and explore other creative avenues.

QI and Beyond:

Despite his declared "retirement" from panel shows, Bill remained a beloved presence on television. He has made countless appearances on the popular quiz show "QI" since its inception in 2003. His insightful contributions and playful banter with host Stephen Fry and fellow panelist Alan Davies cemented him as a fan favorite. Interestingly, Bill was even the winner of the show's unaired pilot episode, showcasing his vast knowledge base and quick wit. His appearances on QI are often characterized by his ability to think outside the box and deliver unexpected answers to seemingly straightforward questions. He can riff on historical trivia, delve into obscure scientific facts, or launch into tangents about obscure musical genres, all delivered with his signature blend of humor and intelligence. Bill's presence on QI has not only entertained viewers but also challenged them to think differently and approach knowledge from a new perspective.

Venturing Beyond Comedy:

Bill's television career wasn't solely focused on comedy. He showcased his dramatic talents with a cameo role in Alan Davies' detective drama series ***"Jonathan Creek."*** He played the delightfully eccentric character Kenny Starkiss, a failing street magician whose flamboyant persona and desperate attempts at grand illusions provided a welcome dose of comedic relief amidst the show's more serious detective work.

Bill's willingness to experiment with different genres extended to sitcoms. He guest-starred in an episode of Sean Lock's "Fifteen Storeys High," a quirky sitcom set in a tower block. While details about his specific role are scant, it likely involved Bill's signature blend of observational humor and offbeat charm. He also appeared on "Friday Night with Jonathan Ross," a popular talk show known for its relaxed atmosphere and witty celebrity interviews. Bill's appearance undoubtedly brought his unique brand of humor and insightful conversation to the show, likely engaging in hilarious banter with host Jonathan Ross and the other celebrity guests.

Bill's television repertoire is not limited to being a guest. In 2011, he hosted his own show, "Comic's Choice," a platform for showcasing up-and-coming comedic talent. This venture demonstrated Bill's passion for nurturing new comedians and giving them a platform to develop their craft. The show featured a variety of rising stars, from observational humorists to musical comedians, and Bill's genuine enthusiasm and comedic expertise created a supportive and encouraging environment for these new voices. "Comic's Choice" highlighted Bill's commitment to the comedic community and his desire to see the genre flourish.

A Wildlife Champion

Bill Bailey's comedic talents extend far beyond laughter. His passion for wildlife conservation led him to "Wild Thing I Love You," a 2006 Channel 4 series focusing on the protection of Britain's native animals. This program showcased Bill's genuine enthusiasm for the natural world as he participated in efforts to rehome badgers, owls, and water voles. The series served as a platform to raise awareness about environmental issues and the importance of protecting endangered species.

Bill's commitment to conservation was not limited to a single show. He has spoken out about the need for environmental protection on numerous occasions, using his platform as a comedian and television personality to advocate for wildlife conservation efforts. Whether it's appearing on nature documentaries or lending his voice to environmental campaigns, Bill's dedication to the natural world is a constant undercurrent throughout his television career.

He ventured into the world of teen drama with a role in the second season of "Skins," a show exploring the lives of a group of teenagers navigating adolescence. Bill played Maxxie's dad, Walter Oliver, a character grappling with his son's aspirations to become a dancer. This role showcased Bill's dramatic range as he portrayed a character with conflicting emotions and traditional expectations.

Bill's television journey continued with a guest appearance on the first episode of "Grand Designs Live," a show exploring innovative and eco-friendly architecture. He joined host Kevin McCloud in the construction of his eco-friendly home, highlighting his interest in sustainability and environmental responsibility.

Natural History Documentaries:

Bill's passion for the natural world continued to blossom with appearances on wildlife documentaries. In 2009, he appeared in the BBC series "Hustle," a show about a group of con artists, but his heart clearly belonged to the natural world. That same year, he presented "Bill Bailey's Birdwatching Bonanza," a program dedicated to the fascinating world of birds. The show explored the unique behaviors and adaptations of various bird species, from the colorful plumage of peacocks to the complex migratory patterns of geese. Bill's infectious enthusiasm and quirky sense of humor made birdwatching seem like an exciting adventure, inspiring audiences to look up and appreciate the avian wonders all around them.

In 2010, Bill further explored wildlife in "Baboons With Bill Bailey," an ITV1 miniseries filmed in Cape Town. This eight-episode series offered viewers a glimpse into the lives of baboons and explored the complex social structures of these intelligent primates. Bill's genuine curiosity and respectful approach to the animals allowed viewers to witness the playful antics of baboon youngsters, the dominance struggles within the troop, and the close relationships between mothers and their babies. The series wasn't just about entertainment; it also served as an educational tool, highlighting the importance of baboon conservation and the threats these primates face in their natural habitat. Bill's natural charisma and engaging narration made "Baboons With Bill Bailey" an informative and entertaining program that appealed to viewers of all ages.

A Trip to Doctor Who:

Bill's diverse television career even landed him a role in the iconic science fiction series "Doctor Who." In the 2011 Christmas special titled "The Doctor, the Widow and the Wardrobe," he portrayed the Harvest Ranger Droxil, who came from the planet Androzani Major. This unexpected cameo showcased Bill's adaptability and his willingness to tackle diverse roles, adding another layer to his impressive television resume. "Doctor

Who" is a long-running British science fiction program following the adventures of the Doctor, a time-traveling alien who explores the universe with companions. The series is known for its blend of humor, adventure, and science fiction themes. Bill's appearance in the Christmas special brought a touch of his signature comedic timing and whimsical charm to the beloved series. While a one-time role, it was a memorable addition to the "Doctor Who" universe and a testament to Bill's ability to connect with audiences across genres.

In Search of Alfred Russel Wallace

Bill Bailey's television journey continues to surprise and delight audiences. His passion for exploration and historical figures led him to delve into the fascinating life of Alfred Russel Wallace, a naturalist who co-discovered the theory of evolution alongside Charles Darwin.

In 2009, Bill presented a travelogue exploring Indonesia, the home of many of Wallace's groundbreaking discoveries. Bill has spoken about feeling a "real affinity" with Wallace, believing him to be somewhat "airbrushed out of history." This project served as a tribute to Wallace's contributions to science and a way to bring his story to a wider audience. Through Bill's engaging narration and exploration of the stunning Indonesian landscapes, viewers gained a deeper appreciation for Wallace's life and work.

Bill's admiration for Wallace stemmed from a shared sense of curiosity and a love for the natural world. Wallace, like Bill, was a keen observer and collector, fascinated by the diversity of life on Earth. Bill's travelogue wasn't just a biographical portrait; it was also a celebration of exploration and scientific discovery. As Bill journeyed through Indonesia, he followed in Wallace's footsteps, visiting the same islands and rainforests that inspired Wallace's groundbreaking theories. The program featured interviews with scientists who discussed Wallace's legacy and the ongoing importance of conservation efforts in Indonesia. Bill's genuine enthusiasm and infectious curiosity were perfectly suited to telling the story of this under-appreciated scientist. He brought Wallace's discoveries to life, highlighting the beauty and complexity of the natural world that Wallace spent his life exploring.

Bill's passion for Wallace culminated in the 2013 BBC Two documentary series "Bill Bailey's Jungle Hero." This two-part program was a chance for Bill to delve deeper into Wallace's life and work. Traveling to Indonesia and Borneo, Bill retraced Wallace's footsteps and explored the diverse ecosystems that inspired his groundbreaking theories. He visited the lush rainforests of the Malay Archipelago, encountering a dazzling array of wildlife, from orangutans swinging through the trees to colorful birds of paradise displaying their plumage. Bill interacted with scientists studying these creatures, learning about their unique adaptations and the threats they face due to habitat loss. The series also explored Wallace's encounters with indigenous communities in Indonesia and Borneo. Bill met with local people who shared their knowledge of the natural world and their traditions of living in harmony with the environment. "Bill Bailey's Jungle Hero" wasn't just a documentary about Alfred Russel Wallace; it was also a celebration of the natural wonders of Southeast Asia and a call to action for conservation.

Strictly Come Dancing: Unexpected Champion

In 2020, Bill took a surprising turn and participated in the 18th season of the popular dance competition "Strictly Come Dancing." Paired with professional dancer Oti Mabuse, a multiple-time champion on the show, Bill defied expectations. With no prior dance experience, Bill showcased his dedication, humor, and surprisingly graceful moves, quickly becoming a fan favorite. His signature comedic timing and quirky charm translated perfectly to the dance floor. He brought a unique energy to his routines, whether it was the elegance of a waltz or the playful fun of a Charleston. The judges, often known for their critiques, were consistently impressed by Bill's progress and his willingness to learn. Week after week, Bill and Oti delivered entertaining and technically impressive routines, captivating audiences with their undeniable chemistry. Bill's journey on "Strictly Come Dancing" was an inspiration to viewers of all ages. It demonstrated that with hard work, dedication, and a positive attitude, anything is possible. Ultimately, Bill and Oti waltzed their way to victory, making Bill the show's oldest winner at the age of 55. This unexpected triumph cemented Bill's status as a national treasure, a comedian who could not only make you laugh but could also surprise you with his talents and determination.

A Voice for Children's Entertainment:

In 2022, Bill lent his voice to the animated Christmas special "The Smeds and The Smoos," an adaptation of the beloved children's book by Julia Donaldson. He voiced Grandfather Smed, adding his unique charm and storytelling skills to this heartwarming tale. This project showcased Bill's versatility as a performer and his ability to connect with audiences of all ages. Bill's warm and engaging voice brought Grandfather Smed to life, perfectly capturing the character's wisdom and kindness. The story itself, which celebrates the importance of friendship and overcoming differences, resonated with children and adults alike. Bill's participation in "The Smeds and The Smoos" not only marked a new chapter in his television career but also demonstrated his commitment to projects that entertain and inspire young viewers.

CHAPTER FOUR

LIVE PERFORMANCES AND TOURS

Bill Bailey is renowned not only for his television and film work but also for his dynamic and innovative live performances. His stand-up comedy tours are celebrated for their unique blend of music, humor, and surreal storytelling, captivating audiences worldwide.

Bailey's journey as a live performer began in the late 1980s and early 1990s when he toured the UK with fellow comedians such as Mark Lamarr. His early performances were characterized by his distinctive style, which combined traditional stand-up comedy with musical parodies and deconstructions of conventional jokes. These early gigs helped Bailey hone his craft and develop the eclectic style that would define his later work.

Music is an integral part of Bill's live experience. He isn't just a comedian with a guitar; he's a multi-instrumentalist who seamlessly weaves music into his act. From the electrifying riffs of his electric guitar solos to the melancholic beauty of his keyboard melodies, Bill's musical talents add another layer of depth and humor to his performances. One iconic moment is his rendition of "Old MacDonald Had a Farm" sung in the style of Tom Waits, transforming a familiar children's song into a darkly comedic masterpiece.

Bill's stand-up routines are far from conventional. He's a master storyteller, weaving tales of his experiences, observations, and flights of fancy. He takes seemingly mundane topics and turns them into hilarious anecdotes. One moment, he'll be recounting a disastrous encounter with a particularly aggressive squirrel in his garden, and the next, he'll be launching into a philosophical treatise on the migratory patterns of the lesser-spotted toaster (yes, you read that right). Bill's stories are peppered with witty observations, absurdist tangents, and unexpected punchlines that leave audiences in stitches. These stories are often punctuated by Bill's signature sound effects and character voices, adding to the visual and auditory feast that is a Bill Bailey live show. A memorable moment might be his exploration of the natural world, complete with bird calls and impersonations of various creatures, all delivered with a straight face that heightens the comedic impact. His ability to find humor in the mundane and elevate the ordinary to the extraordinary is a hallmark of his live performances

Bill thrives on audience interaction. He doesn't just tell jokes; he engages the crowd, inviting them to participate in his comedic tapestry. He might pick unsuspecting audience members to play roles in his outlandish scenarios, have them provide sound effects for his musical numbers, or launch into improvised conversations that veer wildly off topic. This audience participation adds an element of unpredictability to the show, ensuring no two Bill Bailey performances are ever exactly the same. Bill's ability to think on his feet and adapt his material to the audience ensures that no two performances are ever the same, keeping the experience fresh and exciting for both the comedian and the crowd.

Bill's live shows are filled with moments that stay with audiences long after the curtain falls. There's the infamous "Flameo Hotman" routine, where Bill attempts (and hilariously fails) to play a ukulele while balancing a flaming baton. There's his exploration of the philosophical musings of a particularly existential slug, pondering the vastness of the universe from the bottom of a flowerpot. And who can forget his epic battles with a rogue microphone stand, a recurring foe in his comedic universe. These moments, both meticulously crafted and delightfully spontaneous, are what make Bill Bailey's live shows so special.

Bill's live shows are more than just stand-up routines; they are theatrical productions. He utilizes lighting, props, and costume changes to create a visually engaging experience. One memorable moment might be his emergence from a giant inflatable badger head, much to the audience's amusement. Another highlight could be his elaborate light show that accompanies a particularly dramatic musical interlude. These theatrical elements add to the overall spectacle of Bill's live shows, creating a sense of wonder and absurdity that keeps his audiences captivated.

Bill Bailey's Tours: A Global Journey of Comedy and Music

Bill Bailey's live tours have been a significant part of his career, showcasing his unique blend of comedy, music, and surreal storytelling to audiences worldwide. His ability to connect with diverse audiences through his eclectic performances has cemented his status as a beloved international comedian.

Bewilderness: A Global Comedy Invasion (2001)

In 2001, Bill embarked on a world tour with ***"Bewilderness,"*** a show that perfectly captured his multifaceted comedic talents. This tour marked a significant turning point in his career, solidifying his reputation as a comedian who could entertain audiences across continents. A recording of a "Bewilderness" performance in Swansea, Wales, was released on DVD in 2001, allowing fans to relive the comedic brilliance of the show even after the tour concluded. The same year, Channel 4 broadcasted a special featuring highlights from the tour, bringing Bill's unique brand of humor to living rooms across the United Kingdom.

"Bewilderness" was not just a European success. Bill successfully adapted the show for American audiences, proving that his humor transcended cultural boundaries. In 2002, he released a CD featuring a recording of a performance at the WestBeth Theatre in New York City. This CD captured the essence of the "Bewilderness" experience, showcasing Bill's musical parodies, witty observations, and signature storytelling.

"Bewilderness" featured some of Bill's most memorable musical moments. Audiences were treated to hilarious song parodies like "Unisex Chip Shop," a clever tribute to the iconic British singer-songwriter Billy Bragg. The show also featured Bill's deconstructions of popular television themes, turning shows like "Countdown" and "The Magic Roundabout" into unexpected sources of comedic fodder. His sharp wit and observational humor resonated with audiences, leaving them both entertained and questioning their own media consumption habits.

The "Bewilderness" tour was not just about live entertainment; it also spawned a successful CD release. Sold outside gigs, the CD featured a mix of studio recordings of songs and monologues previously performed by Bill. This compilation, later released in shops under the title "Bill Bailey: The Ultimate Collection... Ever!", allowed fans to own a piece of the "Bewilderness" experience even if they had not attended the live shows.

While touring with "Bewilderness," Bill showcased his versatility by presenting a Channel 4 countdown show titled "Top Ten Prog Rock." This program, infused with his characteristic humor, explored the world of progressive rock music, a genre known for its intricate arrangements and long instrumental sections. Bill's comedic take on prog rock classics was a treat for fans of the genre and a hilarious introduction for those unfamiliar with its quirks.

Part Troll: Critical Acclaim and Global Recognition (2003)

In 2003, Bill premiered his critically acclaimed show "Part Troll" at the prestigious Edinburgh Festival Fringe. This show marked a turning point in his career. It received rave reviews from critics and audiences alike, solidifying his position as a comedic force to be reckoned with.

The success of "Part Troll" was not confined to the Edinburgh Festival Fringe. Bill transferred the show to London's West End, the heart of British theater. Tickets sold out within a staggering 24 hours, forcing the addition of more dates to meet the phenomenal demand.

"Part Troll" was not just a domestic success. Bill embarked on a global tour with the show, captivating audiences in Australia, New Zealand, and the United States. His ability to adapt his material to different cultural contexts, while retaining his signature comedic style, cemented his reputation as a global comedic icon.

Bill addressed complex issues like the war on Iraq, using humor to provoke thought and spark conversation. He also explored the theme of drugs, engaging in audience interaction by asking them to name different ways of baking cannabis. This willingness to explore sensitive topics, while maintaining a respectful and humorous approach, resonated with audiences looking for a comedian who challenged the status quo.

One of the standout routines in Part Troll involved Bailey asking the audience to name different ways of baking cannabis. This interactive segment not only entertained but also showcased Bailey's ability to engage directly with his audience in a humorous and relatable manner. In 2004, Part Troll was released on DVD, capturing the energy and humor of Bailey's live performances. The DVD release allowed fans to relive the experience and introduced new audiences to his work.

Bill Bailey's Cosmic Jam (2005)

In 2005, Bill treated fans to a blast from the past with the release of "Bill Bailey's Cosmic Jam," a two-disc set featuring his classic 1995 show. This show, a fan favorite, offered a glimpse into Bill's early comedic style and the themes that would remain cornerstones of his humor throughout his career.

The "Bill Bailey's Cosmic Jam" release was not just a nostalgic trip down memory lane. It also included a special director's cut of "Bewilderness." This extended version featured a hilarious routine centered around Stephen Hawking's groundbreaking book "A Brief History of Time." This routine, not included in the original broadcast or DVD release, offered a further glimpse into Bill's ability to blend scientific concepts with his signature comedic wit.

Steampunk at the Edinburgh Festival Fringe (2006)

In 2006, Bill Bailey returned to the prestigious Edinburgh Festival Fringe with a new and innovative show titled Steampunk. This performance was a significant entry in his career, reflecting his continual evolution as a comedian and musician. The show exemplified Bailey's unique ability to blend different genres and themes into a cohesive and entertaining experience.

The title Steampunk refers to a subgenre of science fiction that combines elements of Victorian-era technology with futuristic innovations, often characterized by steam-powered machinery and anachronistic inventions. Bailey used this aesthetic as a backdrop for his performance, creating a visually rich and imaginative setting for his comedy. The steampunk theme allowed Bailey to explore a variety of topics, from historical anachronisms to speculative future technologies, all while maintaining his trademark humor and wit.

Bailey's storytelling in Steampunk was characterized by his whimsical and surreal style. He created intricate and often absurd narratives that captivated the audience, weaving together elements of fantasy, history, and speculative fiction. His ability to switch seamlessly between storytelling and musical performance added a dynamic and engaging layer to the show.

Beautiful Days and Sold-Out Arenas: The Tinselworm Tour (2007)

In 2007, Bill joined the lineup for the renowned Beautiful Days festival, known for its eclectic mix of music and arts. His presence at the festival further solidified his appeal to a diverse audience who appreciated his comedic talent beyond the confines of traditional stand-up. The festival's focus on environmental and social activism also likely resonated with Bill, given his own passions for wildlife conservation and environmental responsibility. Sharing the stage with a variety of musical acts, from up-and-coming indie bands to legendary rock veterans, Bill would have brought a unique comedic energy to the festival, offering audiences a welcome respite from the musical performances.

The same year, Bill embarked on his ambitious "Tinselworm" tour, playing to sold-out crowds across the UK and Europe. The culmination of the tour was a triumphant performance at Wembley Arena, a legendary venue that has hosted some of the biggest names in music and entertainment. This achievement showcased the immense popularity Bill had achieved through his live shows. The massive scale of the Wembley Arena performance presented a unique challenge for Bill. He would have had to adapt his usual stage presence and comedic delivery to fill the expansive venue and ensure that his humor resonated with everyone in the audience, from those seated in the front row to those perched in the farthest reaches of the arena. Bill likely relied on his signature blend of music, storytelling, and audience interaction to create a truly unforgettable comedic experience for his Wembley audience.

Unique Aspects of Bill Bailey's Tours
Musical Integration

Bailey's tours are characterized by his seamless integration of music into his comedy. He performs complex musical pieces using a variety of instruments, including the keyboard, guitar, theremin, and even unconventional ones like the Swiss alpine horn. His musical talent adds depth to his performances and allows him to explore a wide range of comedic themes.

Surreal and Absurd Humor

Bailey's comedy often delves into the surreal and absurd, with routines that challenge conventional logic and explore imaginative scenarios. His whimsical storytelling and unique perspective on everyday topics make his live shows distinctive and engaging.

Interactive Elements

Bailey frequently incorporates interactive elements into his performances, encouraging audience participation and creating a dynamic and unpredictable live experience. This engagement enhances the connection between Bailey and his audience, making each show unique.

Social and Political Commentary

Throughout his tours, Bailey has incorporated social and political commentary into his routines. His ability to address contemporary issues with humor and insight adds an extra layer of relevance and depth to his performances.

Multimedia Use

Bailey often utilizes multimedia elements in his shows, including projected images, videos, and animations that complement his routines. These visual aids create a more immersive experience for the audience and allow Bailey to explore more complex comedic ideas.

CHAPTER FIVE

PERSONAL LIFE

Bill Bailey has been married to Kristin since 1998. Bill's love story with Kristin, is as unique as the man himself. In 1998, while traveling through Asia, they found themselves in Banda, Indonesia. Captivated by the idyllic location, with a stunning lagoon, a smoking volcano, and remnants of a colonial past, Bill and Kristin decided to tie the knot right then and there. This impulsive act of matrimony perfectly embodies Bill's free spirit and his appreciation for the unexpected. Kristin, a former costume designer, has become Bill's pillar of support. She now manages his business affairs, allowing him to focus on his creative endeavors. In 2003, their son Dax was born, adding a new chapter to Bill's life. He often speaks about the joy and perspective that parenthood has brought him.

Hobbies and Interests

A Passion for Nature: The Call of the Wild and the Beauty of Birds

Bill is a dedicated advocate for environmental causes. This passion stems from a deep love for nature and a genuine interest in wildlife. When he is not performing, he might be found birdwatching, a pastime that allows him to connect with the natural world and observe the beauty and complexity of avian life.

Music: A Lifelong Passion

Music is an integral part of Bill's comedic identity. However, his passion for music extends far beyond the quirky songs he performs on stage. He is a talented multi-instrumentalist, adept at playing keyboards, guitars, and even the occasional melodica. When he's not writing comedic songs, he might be found refining his musical skills, composing original pieces, or simply jamming along to his favorite tunes. Music likely serves as a creative outlet for him, a way to express himself beyond the confines of stand-up comedy. Imagine Bill relaxing at home, strumming his guitar and composing a hauntingly beautiful melody, a stark contrast to the silly songs he performs on stage.

He is a multi-instrumentalist, proficient in playing a wide array of instruments including the guitar, keyboard, theremin, kazoo, and bongos. His love for music is not just a hobby but a central part of his identity, seamlessly integrated into his comedy routines.

His talent for music extends beyond performance; he is classically trained and achieved Grade 6 in Clarinet. This formal training underpins his ability to create sophisticated musical parodies and compositions that resonate with his audiences.

Paddleboarding

Bill is an active individual who enjoys outdoor pursuits. One of his hobbies is stand-up paddleboarding (SUP). This activity allows him to combine his love for nature with a healthy dose of exercise. Picture Bill gliding serenely across a tranquil lake on his SUP board, taking in the scenery and enjoying the peace and quiet. This outdoor activity likely provides Bill with a much-needed escape from the hustle and bustle of his comedic career, allowing him to recharge and refocus his creative energy.

Championing British Canoeing: A Supporter of Aquatic Activities

Bill's passion for water extends beyond stand-up paddleboarding. He's an active supporter of British Canoeing, the national governing body for paddlesports in the UK. His support for this organization highlights his appreciation for water-based activities and his desire to promote healthy outdoor pursuits. His involvement with British Canoeing showcases his commitment to promoting healthy living and his dedication to supporting organizations that share his passion for the outdoors.

A Life of Exploration and Discovery

Bill Bailey's hobbies and interests paint a picture of a man who thrives on exploration and discovery. His love for nature, music, languages, and outdoor activities fuels his creativity and adds depth to his comedic persona. These passions allow him to connect with audiences on a deeper level, as they see a glimpse of the man beyond the jokes and quirky musical interludes.

Travel and Adventure

Bailey's love for travel and adventure is well-documented. His spontaneous decision to marry his wife Kristin while traveling in Indonesia epitomizes his adventurous spirit. This passion for exploring new places and cultures often influences his comedy, providing rich material for his routines. His travels around the world, whether for performances or personal leisure, allow him to gather diverse experiences and perspectives, enriching his comedic narrative.

Science Fiction and Star Trek

Bailey is a self-described avid fan of Star Trek, a passion that aligns with his broader love for science fiction. This interest often finds its way into his comedy routines, where he references the iconic series, much to the delight of his audience.

His knowledge of Star Trek and its themes adds depth to his comedic material, allowing him to connect with fellow sci-fi enthusiasts and explore complex topics in a humorous way.

Love for Football

Bailey is an ardent supporter of Queens Park Rangers (QPR), a football club based in West London. His dedication to the team goes beyond mere fandom; it is a significant aspect of his personal life. His passion for football is often reflected in his comedy, where he shares humorous anecdotes and insights related to the sport. This enthusiasm for football provides a relatable and humanizing aspect to his public persona.

Bill Bailey's Political Views

Bill Bailey has been a lifelong supporter of the Labour Party, a political stance that reflects his commitment to social justice, equality, and progressive policies. His dedication to the party has been evident throughout his career, as he frequently voices his support for Labour's ideals and initiatives. His endorsement of the Labour Party is not merely a casual preference but a deeply held conviction that aligns with his personal values and vision for society.

Bailey actively participated in the Labour Party's campaign for the 2010 general election. He appeared in the party's fifth election broadcast, using his platform to advocate for Labour's policies and to reach a broader audience. His involvement in the campaign demonstrated his willingness to engage directly in the political process and his belief in the importance of political activism.

In 2015, Bailey endorsed Jeremy Corbyn's campaign during the Labour Party leadership election. His endorsement was rooted in his admiration for Corbyn's straightforward and principled approach to politics. Bailey stated, "Corbyn's nomination showed there is a kind of craving for a bit of honest speaking, a bit of principled plain speaking." This sentiment highlights Bailey's appreciation for integrity and authenticity in political leadership. While supporting Corbyn, Bailey also acknowledged the challenges the leader faced. He noted that Corbyn was in "a bit of a bind" due to the need to navigate a "toxic political atmosphere."

Philanthropy and Activism

Advocacy for Gender Equality and Feminism

Bill Bailey is an ardent feminist and a staunch supporter of the Fawcett Society, an organization dedicated to promoting gender equality and women's rights. The Fawcett Society works to close the gender pay gap, combat discrimination, and advocate for policies that support women's advancement in various spheres of life.

Bailey's involvement with the Fawcett Society underscores his commitment to feminist principles and his recognition of the importance of addressing systemic gender inequalities. His support helps to amplify the organization's efforts and bring greater attention to the cause of gender equality.

Advocacy for Men's Health Issues

Prostate Cancer Awareness

Bailey is a prominent advocate for men's health issues, with a particular focus on raising awareness about prostate cancer. Prostate cancer is a significant health concern for men, and early detection and treatment are crucial for improving outcomes.

By using his platform to highlight the importance of regular screenings and early detection, Bailey contributes to public awareness and encourages men to take proactive steps in managing their health.

Men United Campaign

In 2014, Bailey spearheaded the launch of "Men United vs. Prostate Cancer." This initiative tackles two crucial aspects of the fight against prostate cancer: raising funds for research and promoting awareness among men at higher risk. By specifically targeting this demographic, Bailey aims to break down barriers and encourage men to prioritize their health.

Through his involvement, Bailey helps to destigmatize conversations about men's health and promotes a culture of support and awareness among men.

His dedication does not stop at raising awareness. Bailey actively participates in fundraising efforts. He recently completed **"Bill's Ridgeway Walk,"** a challenging trek designed to raise money for cancer research through Stand Up To Cancer. This personal commitment sets a powerful example and inspires others to take action.

Animal Welfare and Environmental Conservation

International Animal Rescue

Bailey is a patron of International Animal Rescue (IAR), an organization committed to rescuing and rehabilitating animals in distress. IAR's work includes campaigns to save endangered species, provide veterinary care, and protect habitats.

One of Bailey's notable contributions to IAR is his involvement in the campaign to rescue dancing bears. These bears, often subjected to cruel treatment and forced to perform for entertainment, are rescued and rehabilitated by IAR. Bailey's support has been instrumental in raising awareness and funds for this cause, helping to end the exploitation of these animals.

Sumatran Orangutan Society

Bailey has also campaigned for the Sumatran Orangutan Society (SOS), an organization dedicated to the conservation of Sumatran orangutans and their habitats. Deforestation and habitat destruction pose significant threats to these critically endangered primates.

Bailey's involvement with SOS highlights his commitment to protecting endangered species and preserving biodiversity. His efforts include fundraising, advocacy, and raising public awareness about the plight of Sumatran orangutans.

Honorary Doctorate in Conservation and Sustainability

In recognition of his contributions to environmental conservation, Bailey received an honorary doctorate in conservation and sustainability from the Australian University of the Sunshine Coast in October 2014. This accolade reflects his significant impact on environmental advocacy and his dedication to promoting sustainable practices.

Bailey's work in conservation extends beyond individual campaigns, encompassing a broader commitment to environmental sustainability and the protection of natural habitats worldwide.

Bill Bailey's philanthropy and activism are characterized by a deep commitment to a variety of causes, including gender equality, men's health, animal welfare, and environmental conservation. His support for the Fawcett Society underscores his dedication to feminist principles and the fight for gender equality. Through his advocacy for prostate cancer awareness and the Men United campaign, Bailey helps to address critical men's health issues and encourages proactive health management.

Bailey's passion for animal welfare is evident in his role as a patron of International Animal Rescue and his campaigns for the Sumatran Orangutan Society. His efforts to rescue dancing bears and protect endangered species highlight his dedication to ending animal exploitation and preserving biodiversity. The honorary doctorate he received for his work in conservation and sustainability further recognizes his significant contributions to environmental advocacy.

Through his diverse philanthropic endeavors, Bailey uses his platform to raise awareness, advocate for change, and inspire others to join him in making a positive impact on the world. His multifaceted activism reflects a holistic approach to addressing some of the most pressing issues of our time, from social justice and health to animal welfare and environmental sustainability.

Wallace Memorial Fund Patron:

Bailey serves as a patron for the Wallace Memorial Fund, a testament to his admiration for the lesser-known naturalist Alfred Russel Wallace. His support helped raise £50,000 for a bronze statue honoring Wallace at the Natural History Museum. At the unveiling, Bailey himself lauded Wallace as a "maverick genius," highlighting the importance of recognizing his groundbreaking discoveries alongside other prominent figures in the scientific field. This act showcases Bailey's appreciation for scientific exploration.

CHAPTER SIX

A CAREER CROWNED WITH RECOGNITION

Bill Bailey's comedic genius and multifaceted talents have garnered him a well-deserved collection of awards and recognition throughout his impressive career.

Time Out Comedy Award (1995) & Perrier Award Nomination (1996):

In 1995, Bailey's comedic talents were acknowledged with a win at the Time Out Comedy Awards, a major award show in London at the time. This recognition was followed by a nomination for the prestigious Perrier Comedy Award (later renamed the Edinburgh Comedy Award) in 1996. While he didn't win the Perrier Award, the nomination itself was a significant mark of recognition. The Perrier Award is considered one of the highest accolades in British stand-up comedy, and a nomination places a comedian in the company of other rising stars and established greats. This early recognition from such a respected award body no doubt boosted Bailey's profile within the comedy industry and helped him gain wider attention. It likely played a role in him landing his own BBC show, "Is It Bill Bailey?" in 1998, which proved to be a significant platform for him to showcase his unique comedic talents to a national audience. The show's success further solidified his reputation as a rising star in British comedy.

British Comedy Award (1999):

Winning the "Best Live Stand-Up" award at the British Comedy Awards in 1999 was a major milestone for Bailey. The British Comedy Awards are considered one of the most prestigious comedy awards in the UK, recognizing excellence in all aspects of British comedy. This win solidified his place as a leading figure in British comedy and helped propel him to even greater success. The award is a testament to his ability to connect with audiences through his unique blend of observational humor, musicality, and intelligent wit.

Channel 4's 100 Greatest Stand-Ups (2007 & 2010):

Being voted one of the "greatest stand-up comics" twice on Channel 4's "100 Greatest Stand-Ups" list is a testament to Bailey's enduring comedic influence. Inclusion on such a prestigious list speaks volumes about the impact he has had on British comedy. This recognition places him amongst comedy legends and ensures his place in the comedy history books. The fact that he was voted onto the list twice, several years apart, highlights the consistency and longevity of his comedic appeal. This achievement is a significant recognition from his peers and the wider comedy industry, solidifying his reputation as a true comedic force.

Chortle Awards

Over the years, Bailey has been nominated multiple times for Chortle Awards, which celebrate the best of stand-up comedy and live performances in the UK. His consistent nominations are a testament to his enduring popularity and impact on the comedy scene.

Honorary Doctorate in Conservation and Sustainability (2014):

This prestigious award from the Australian University of the Sunshine Coast acknowledges Bailey's dedication to environmental causes that goes beyond simply lending his name to a worthy organization. His influence extends far deeper. Bailey has actively campaigned for conservation efforts, raising awareness about critical issues and inspiring others to take action. This doctorate recognizes not just his comedic achievements but also his commitment to environmental well-being and serves as a testament to the well-rounded nature of his contributions to society.

Bill Bailey's Influence on British Comedy and Stand-Up Culture

Bill Bailey has had a profound and lasting impact on British comedy and stand-up culture. His unique blend of musical talent, surreal humor, and incisive social commentary has distinguished him as one of the most innovative and influential comedians of his generation.

Integration of Music and Comedy

Stand-up comedy traditionally relied solely on spoken word humor. Bailey shattered this mold by seamlessly integrating music into his act. He plays a variety of instruments, from guitar and piano to more unconventional choices like the theremin and the stylophone, creating a dynamic and engaging performance. This innovation not only entertains the audience but also adds another layer of humor to his act. Imagine a comedian setting up a joke about the mundane task of mowing the lawn, and then launching into a quirky keyboard solo to represent the rhythmic whirring of the lawnmower.

This unexpected integration of music can heighten the humor and leave a lasting impression on the audience. Bailey's success with musical comedy has likely inspired other comedians to explore new avenues of expression within stand-up. We've seen comedians incorporate singing, rapping, or even beatboxing into their routines, adding a fresh dimension to their comedic arsenal.

Observational Humor with a Twist:

Bailey excels at observational humor, finding humor in the everyday. However, he doesn't stop there. He injects his observations with a healthy dose of absurdity, creating surreal scenarios and characters that elevate his humor to a new level. This playful exploration of the absurd can be seen in his riffs on mundane topics like traffic jams or office life. He might describe a traffic jam as a "metropolitan centipede," inching its way through the urban jungle. Or, he might portray a particularly soul-crushing office meeting as a gathering of existential zombies. This unexpected twist on the familiar catches the audience off guard and forces them to see the world in a new, funnier light. Bailey's influence can be seen in the work of comedians like Tim Key and Alice Fraser, who also like to weave absurdity into their observational humor. Their deadpan delivery and bizarre scenarios owe a debt to Bailey's ability to find humor in the unexpected and elevate the ordinary to the extraordinary.

Intelligence on Stage

Bailey's jokes often tap into a wide range of knowledge, from music and science to philosophy and current affairs. This intellectual depth appeals to a broad audience and challenges the notion that comedy needs to be simplistic. His success with this approach may have encouraged other comedians to integrate more intellectual humor into their sets. This can manifest in several ways. Some comedians, like Ricky Gervais, might use their stand-up routines to explore philosophical questions about life and death. Others, like Dara Ó

Briain, might weave scientific facts and historical references into their jokes. By incorporating intellectual humor, these comedians broaden the appeal of stand-up, attracting audiences who appreciate not just laughter, but also a mental workout. Bailey's influence can also be seen in the rise of podcast comedy, where comedians have more time to delve into complex topics in a humorous way.

A Master of Theatricality

Bailey elevates his stand-up into a theatrical experience. He uses costumes, props, and physical comedy to create a visually engaging performance. For instance, he might don a flamboyant costume to embody an eccentric character he's created, or use a toy car to hilariously depict a traffic jam. This theatricality injects energy and dynamism into his act, keeping the audience on the edge of their seats. Bailey's influence can be seen in the work of comedians like Phil Wang and Jamie Demetriou, who incorporate costume changes, elaborate set design, and audience interaction into their routines. These theatrical elements transform their stand-up sets into full-fledged comedic productions.

Comedy with a Message:

While primarily a comedian, Bailey does not shy away from tackling social and environmental issues. He weaves these themes into his act in a way that is both funny and thought-provoking. For example, he might riff on the absurdity of climate change denial through a musical parody, or use his stand-up routine to raise awareness about the plight of endangered species. This approach challenges the notion that stand-up comedy should be purely entertainment, and demonstrates its potential as a platform for social commentary. Bailey's influence can be seen in the rise of comedians like Nish Kumar and Frankie Boyle, who use their humor to skewer political hypocrisy and social injustice. Their work demonstrates the power of stand-up comedy to not only make us laugh, but also to make us think critically about the world around us.

Advocacy Through Comedy

Bailey uses his platform to advocate for various causes, including animal rights, environmental conservation, and men's health issues. By incorporating these themes into his comedy, he raises awareness and encourages his audience to think critically about these issues.

His advocacy has inspired other comedians to use their influence for social and political activism, contributing to a broader trend of socially conscious comedy.

CHAPTER SEVEN

QUOTES AND CAPTIVATING FACTS

Over the years, he has shared numerous quotes that reflect his comedic style, philosophical musings, and social commentary.

"Life is a series of increasingly expensive disappointments." - This quote captures the bittersweet reality of life, where aspirations often collide with harsh realities. Delivered in Bailey's signature deadpan style, it resonates with anyone who's ever felt like life isn't quite living up to the hype.

"A perfect example of how not to solve a problem: throwing a jumper over it." - This nonsensical image perfectly encapsulates the absurdity of some solutions we encounter in life. It's a reminder to sometimes step back and question the logic behind things.

"If you're looking for a metaphor for the meaning of life, don't look at me. I'm here to talk about moths." - This self-deprecating humor acknowledges the grand questions of life while simultaneously highlighting the beauty of focusing on the smaller, often overlooked things like moths.

"I like to think of the internet as a giant filing cabinet full of old crisp packets." - This witty comparison captures the vastness and disorganized nature of the internet, where valuable information can be buried under a mountain of irrelevant content.

"There's a fine line between genius and insanity. I don't think there's a fine line, I actually think there's a chasm." - This playful observation on the nature of genius pokes fun at the sometimes-unpredictable nature of creative minds.

"Contentment is knowing you are right. Happiness is knowing." - This quote offers a philosophical twist on happiness. It suggests that true happiness comes from experiencing the world with all its complexities, not just clinging to personal convictions.

"Life is absurd, and sometimes the only way to make sense of it is through laughter." - Bailey often embraces the absurdity of life in his comedy, using humor as a way to navigate and understand the complexities of existence.

" Our existence is simply a fleeting blip in the vast and enigmatic universe. We should make the most of it." - Reflecting on the fleeting nature of life, Bailey encourages living fully and appreciating the wonders of the universe.

"The natural world is a chaotic, beautiful, messy, unpredictable thing. It's like a giant malfunctioning filing cabinet full of wonderful, strange creatures."

" If we continue to treat our planet like a disposable lighter, we will ultimately run out of flint."

"Sometimes the best ideas come when you're doing something else entirely. Like, for example, while you're watching paint dry."

"Music is a universal language. Unfortunately, it translates to 'turn it down' in most places."

Captivating Facts About Bill Bailey

From Rock Dreams to Stand-Up Stardom:

Did you know Bailey once harbored rockstar aspirations? He reminisced in a Guardian interview about his early band, "Behind Closed Doors," and their first public gig. While the solo might not have gone exactly as planned, it marked a turning point, showcasing his early foray into musical performance, later channeled into his unique comedic style.

Classically Trained Musician:

Bill Bailey is a classically trained musician with a remarkable talent for various instruments. He is known for playing the piano, guitar, keyboards, theremin, kazoo, and bongos, among others. He achieved Grade 6 in Clarinet and has perfect pitch, which he often demonstrates in his performances.

Nickname Origin

The nickname "Bill" was given to him by his music teacher at King Edward's School in Bath, who was impressed with his rendition of the song "Won't You Come Home Bill Bailey" on the guitar.

Academic Prowess

Bailey was an academically gifted student and the only pupil at his school to study A-level music, which he passed with an A grade. He was also the captain of the KES 2nd XI cricket team in 1982.

Early TV Appearance

One of Bailey's earliest television appearances was on the children's show "Motormouth" in the late 1980s, where he played the piano for a mind-reading dog.

Breakthrough and Success

Bailey achieved significant recognition for his role as Manny Bianco in the Channel 4 sitcom "Black Books." The show, created by and starring Dylan Moran, became a cult classic and showcased Bailey's talent for acting and comedy.

A Bug for Entomology:

Beyond his comedic facade, he harbors a genuine fascination with insects, particularly moths. This scientific curiosity occasionally surfaces in his humor, adding an unexpected layer of intellectual wit to his jokes.

Passion for Wildlife and Birdwatching

Bill Bailey's love for nature is not just a casual hobby but a profound passion. He is an avid birdwatcher and has been involved in various conservation projects. His enthusiasm for wildlife has led him to explore and support numerous initiatives aimed at protecting natural habitats and preserving biodiversity.

Bailey's commitment to the environment extends to active participation in wildlife conservation efforts. He supports organizations and campaigns focused on protecting endangered species and promoting ecological sustainability. His work with the International Animal Rescue and the Sumatran Orangutan Society highlights his dedication to these causes.

Fluency in Multiple Languages

Bill Bailey is impressively multilingual, with fluency in French and German. This linguistic talent not only enhances his ability to connect with a broader audience during international performances but also adds a unique dimension to his comedic repertoire.

His proficiency in multiple languages allows Bailey to perform and interact with fans across different countries more effectively. This skill has contributed to his global appeal and success, making his shows accessible and relatable to a diverse audience.

Avid User of Social Media

In the digital age, Bill Bailey has embraced social media platforms like Twitter and Instagram to stay connected with his fans. He regularly shares updates, behind-the-scenes insights, and humorous content, engaging with his audience in a personal and interactive way.

Published Author

Expanding his creative pursuits beyond comedy and music, Bill Bailey has written and published a book titled "Bill Bailey's Remarkable Guide to British Birds." This informative and humorous guide reflects his deep love for nature and showcases his unique ability to blend comedy with educational content.

Exceptional Improvisation

One of the hallmarks of Bill Bailey's performances is his exceptional improvisational skill. He has an uncanny ability to adapt to unexpected moments on stage, creating spontaneous and memorable comedic moments that captivate audiences.

CONCLUSION

Bill Bailey stands as a singular figure in the world of entertainment, blending an array of talents and interests into a unique and compelling career. His journey from a young boy in Bath, England, captivated by music and performance, to a globally recognized comedian, musician, and actor, is a testament to his extraordinary abilities and relentless pursuit of artistic expression.

Bailey's versatility is one of his most defining characteristics. He has seamlessly integrated music, comedy, and acting into a career that defies easy categorization. As a classically trained musician with a knack for comedic timing, Bailey has created a distinctive niche in the entertainment industry. His live performances are renowned for their spontaneity, musicality, and wit, leaving audiences both entertained and intellectually stimulated.

His diverse musical skillset, ranging from keyboards and guitars to theremins, kazoos, and bongos, is a clear sign of his profound talent and dedication. Bailey's performances are a symphony of comedic and musical genius. His ability to blend genres, from jazz and rock to classical and drum'n'bass, and incorporate them into his comedy routines is unparalleled. His improvisational skills and perfect pitch add an extra layer of brilliance to his live shows, making each performance a unique experience.

Bailey's impact on British comedy and stand-up culture cannot be overstated. His innovative approach to humor, which includes deconstructing traditional jokes and integrating surreal and whimsical elements, has influenced a generation of comedians. His television work, particularly his role as Manny Bianco in the beloved sitcom "Black Books," has cemented his status as a cultural icon. Shows like "Is It Bill Bailey?" and his many appearances on panel shows such as "Have I Got News For You" demonstrate his quick intellect and smart humor.

Beyond the stage and screen, Bailey's personal interests and advocacy work paint a picture of a man deeply committed to various causes. His passion for wildlife and birdwatching, multilingual abilities, and engagement with social media illustrate a multifaceted personality. As an advocate for environmental conservation and men's health issues, Bailey has used his platform to raise awareness and support for important causes. His honorary doctorate in conservation and sustainability underscores his dedication to making a positive impact on the world.

Bailey's legacy is one of creativity, intelligence, and humor. His ability to cross boundaries between music, comedy, and acting has set him apart as a true renaissance man of entertainment. Whether performing to a sold-out crowd, advocating for environmental causes, or sharing insights on social media, Bailey remains a dynamic and influential figure. His work continues to inspire and entertain, leaving an indelible mark on the world of comedy and beyond

Bailey's journey exemplifies the value of lifelong learning. From his musical talents to his scientific curiosity and love for languages, he continuously expands his horizons. This constant exploration fuels his creativity, leading him to write a book and even conquer the dance floor on "Strictly Come Dancing."

Bill Bailey is a true entertainer in the fullest sense of the word. He is a comedian who makes us think, a musician who entertains us, and a voice for positive change. His captivating performances, his relentless dedication to his passions, and his genuine connection with his audience solidify his position as a unique and influential figure in British comedy and beyond. His legacy will likely continue to inspire future generations of comedians, musicians, environmentalists, and anyone who dares to embrace their multifaceted selves.

Printed in Great Britain
by Amazon